Timelines, Timelines, Timelines!

by Kelly Boswell

A+ Books are published by Capstone Press,
1710 Roe Crest Drive, North Mankato, Minnesota 56003
www.capstonepub.com

Library of Congress Cataloging-in-Publication Data
Boswell, Kelly.
Timelines, timelines, timelines! / by Kelly Boswell.
  pages cm. — (A+ books: displaying information)
  Includes index.
  Summary: "Introduces types of timelines and how they are used"—Provided by
publisher.
  ISBN 978-1-4765-0261-8 (library binding)
  ISBN 978-1-4765-3338-4 (paperback)
  ISBN 978-1-4765-3342-1 (ebook PDF)
1. Chronology—Juvenile literature. 2. Time—Juvenile literature. 3. Calendar—Juvenile
literature. 4. Time measurements—Juvenile literature. I. Title.
  CE13.B67 2014
  529—dc23   2012050520

Editorial Credits
Kristen Mohn, editor; Juliette Peters, designer; Marcie Spence, media researcher;
Charmaine Whitman, production specialist

Photo Credits
iStockphoto: dvdwinters, 19 (bottom); Capstone Studio: Karon Dubke, 1, 3, 4 (right), 5, 6–7,
8, 9, 10, 11, 12, 13, 14, 15, 16, 17, 18–19 (background), 18 (top and bottom), 20–21, 22, 23, 24,
25 (top), 26, 27, 28, 29, 32; Shutterstock: Alena Brozova, cover (middle), Elena Zajchikova,
8–9 (background), Kati Neudert, 6 (left), medvedikov, 25 (bottom), Monkey Business
Images, 18 (middle), robert_s, cover (bottom), sagir, 4 (left), sonya etchison, 19, (top)
Yasonya, cover (top)

Note to Parents, Teachers, and Librarians
This Displaying Information book uses full color photographs and a nonfiction format
to introduce the concept of timelines. This book is designed to be read aloud to a
pre-reader or to be read independently by an early reader. Photographs help listeners
and early readers understand the text and concepts discussed. The book encourages
further learning by including the following sections: Table of Contents, Glossary, Read
More, Internet Sites, and Index. Early readers may need assistance using these features.

Printed in the United States of America in North Mankato, Minnesota.
032013   007223CGF13

Table of Contents

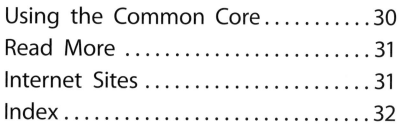

What Is a Timeline?

A timeline is a chart that tells a story.

It shows a set of events and in what order they happened. It also shows how much time passed between each event.

Common Toys

1900s

1800s

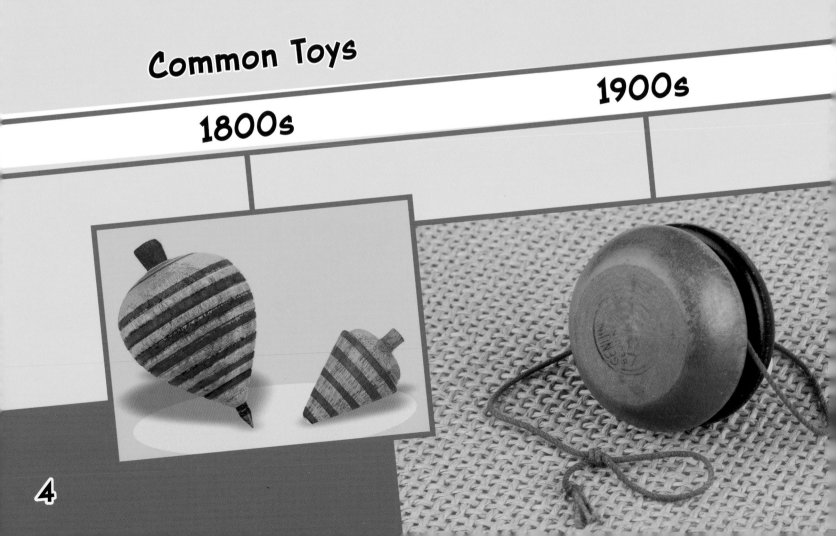

2000s

You can make a timeline of events from long ago. Or you can make a timeline of what happens every day.

Picture Timelines

Deon wants to make a timeline of his day. He asked his dad to take a picture of each thing he does. Deon wakes up, eats breakfast, gets dressed, and goes to school.

When Deon gets home, he has a snack and plays outside. Then it is time for dinner, homework, brushing his teeth, and bed. What a busy day!

Deon looks at his pictures. He draws a line that stands for time. He puts the pictures in the order that the events happened.

Waking up comes first.

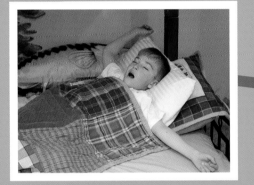

wake up
7:00 am

go to school
8:30 am

play with brother
after school
3:30 pm

Going to bed comes last.

homework
after dinner
7:00 pm

brush teeth
8:15 pm

bedtime
8:30 pm

He writes times below each picture to show when each event happened. Now Deon can see his whole day!

Vertical Timelines

Anna is growing up.

She can ride a bike and tie her shoes.

Anna and her mom have a timeline to keep track of the special things that Anna has done.

A vertical timeline goes up and down.

Anna's timeline begins at the bottom, when she was a baby. Each year the timeline gets taller, just like Anna!

Anna's Timeline

rides a bike— June 2013

ties shoes—August 2012

writes name—July 2011

counts to 10—June 2010

learns colors—January 2010

first words—February 2009

first steps—December 2008

Anna's mom writes the date next to the words that tell what Anna did. The timeline helps them remember these important events.

Horizontal Timelines

January · February · March · April · May · June · July · August · September · Octobe

Anna and her friends were all born in the same year. They find their birthdays on the calendar. Jay's birthday is in September. Lucia's is in May, and Sara was born in June.

Anna's birthday is in March.

Sunday	Monday	Tuesday	Wednesday	Thursday	Friday	Saturday
	1	2	3	4	5	6
7	8	9	10	11	12	13
14	15	16	17	18	19	20
21	22	23	24	25	26	27
28	29	30	31			

Who is the oldest?

Let's use a timeline to find out. We put the months in a horizontal line, which goes sideways. January is the first month of the year. December comes last.

The friends place their names below their birthday month.

July   August   September   October   November   December

Jay

Anna is the oldest.
Who is the youngest?

15

Circle Timelines

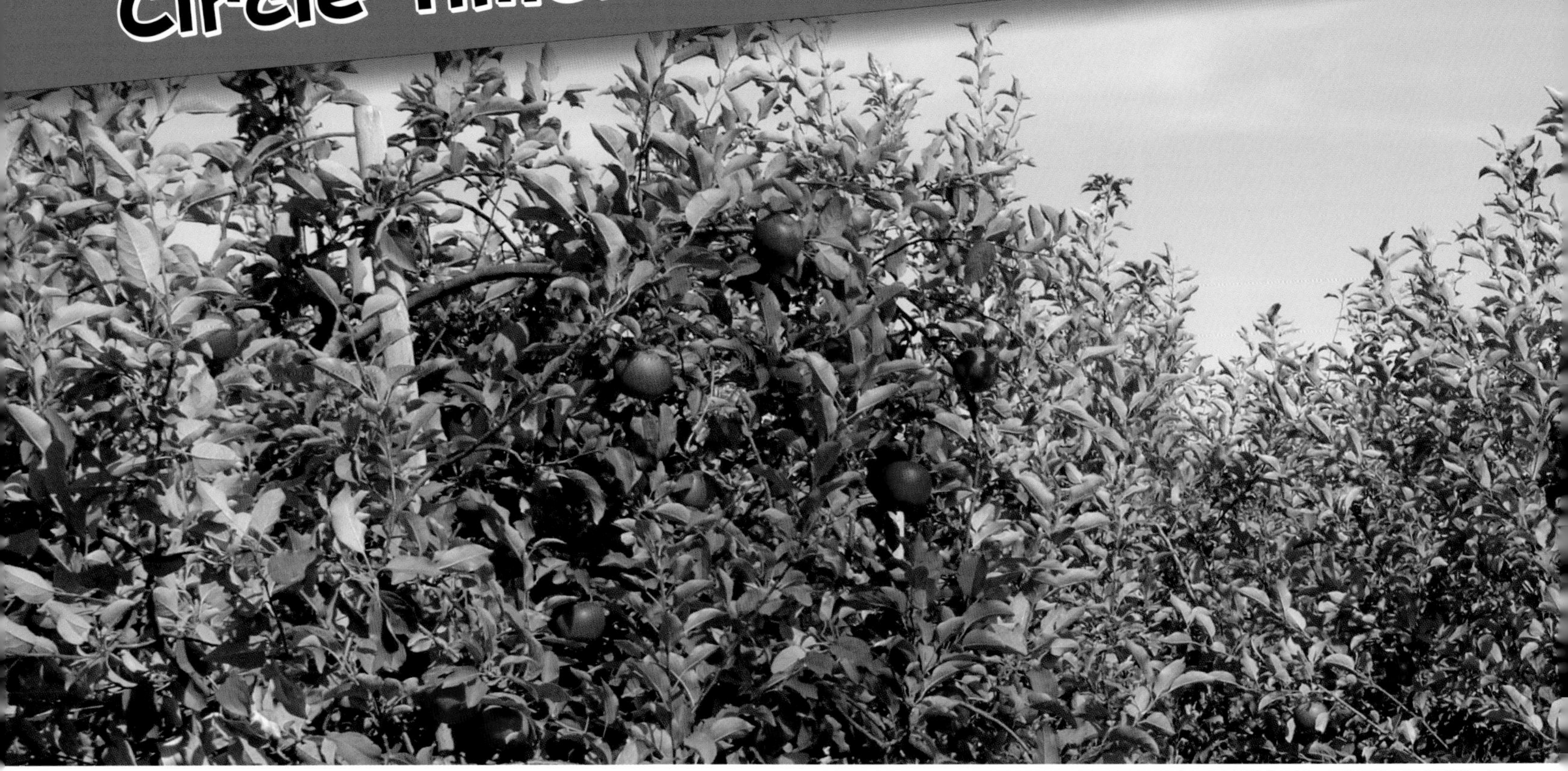

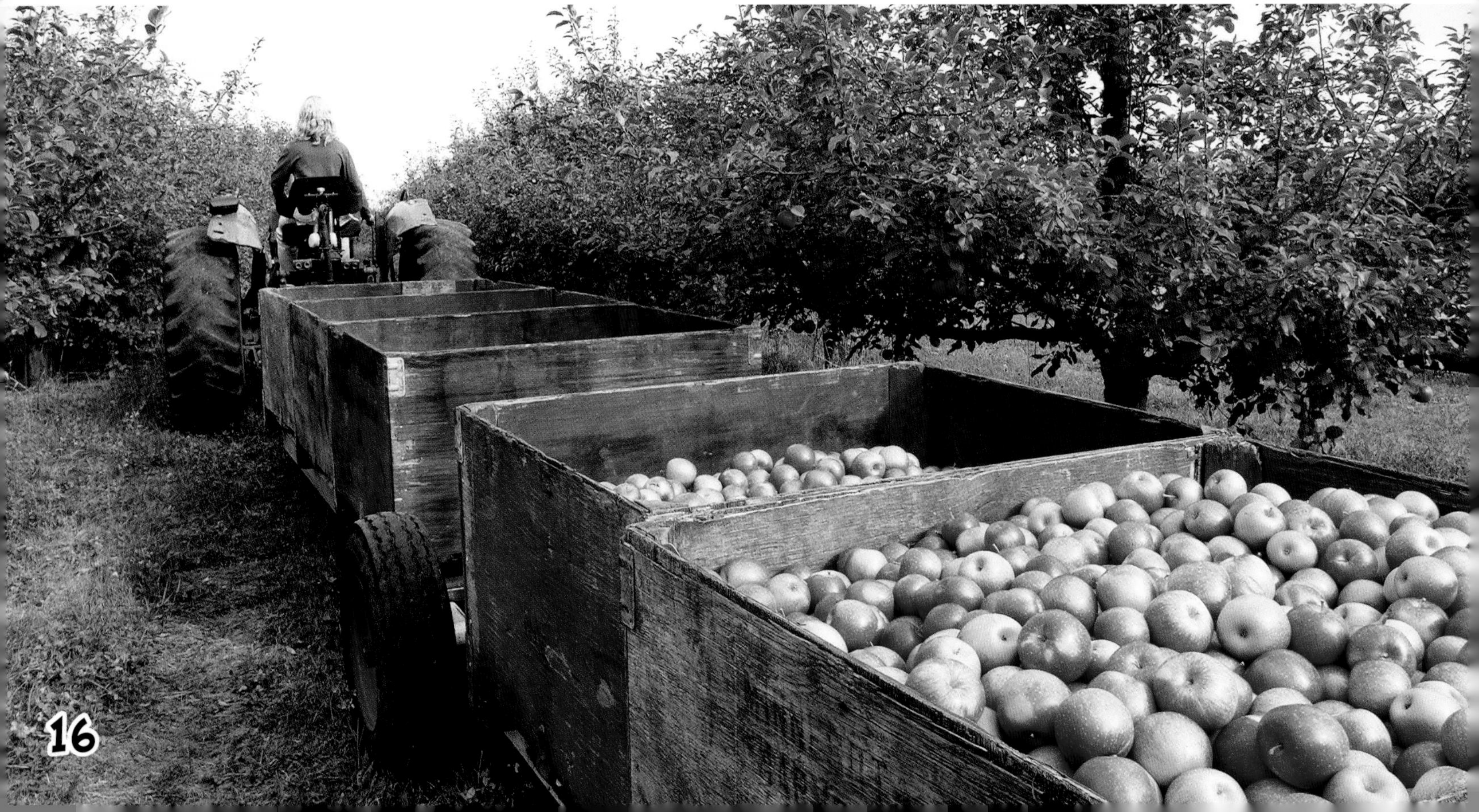

It's time for a field trip!

Mr. Smith's class takes a bus to the apple orchard. The students pick apples, ride in a hay wagon, and bob for apples.

After a picnic lunch, they ride the bus back to school.

The students make a circle timeline to tell about their trip. A circle timeline shows a journey that ends in the same place it began.

start

end

The field trip timeline begins and ends at school. The rest of the circle shows all of the things the children did in between.

Map Timelines

We can also use a map to make a timeline of the field trip. This map shows when and where each event happened.

10:00 Bus

12:15 Bus

11:30 Apple Bobbing

11:45 Picnic

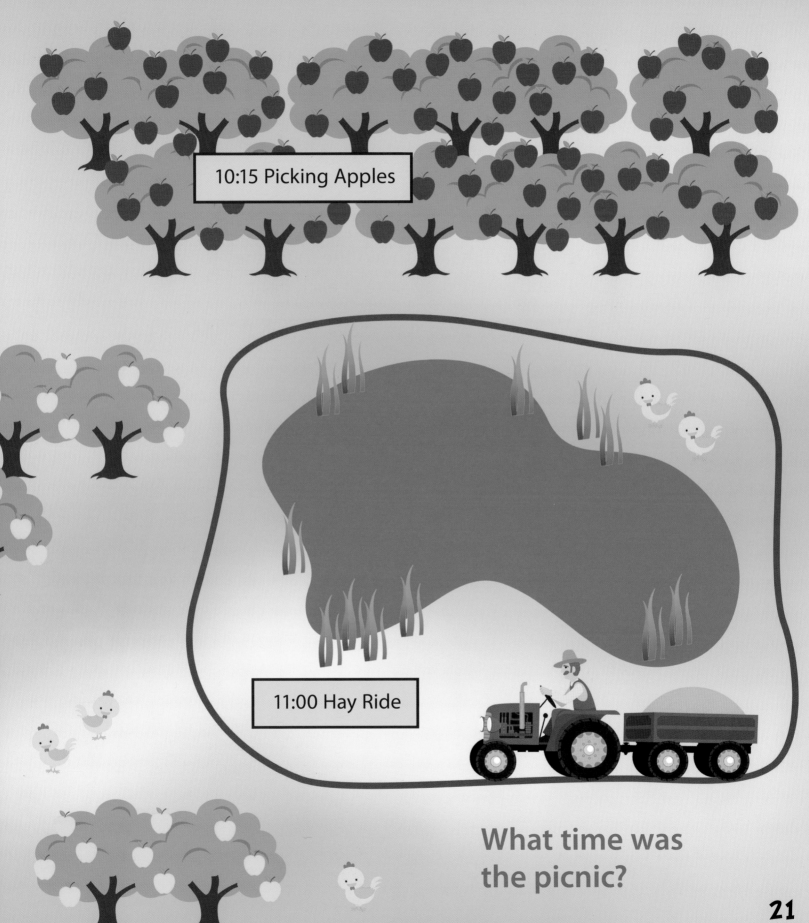

10:15 Picking Apples

11:00 Hay Ride

What time was
the picnic?

21

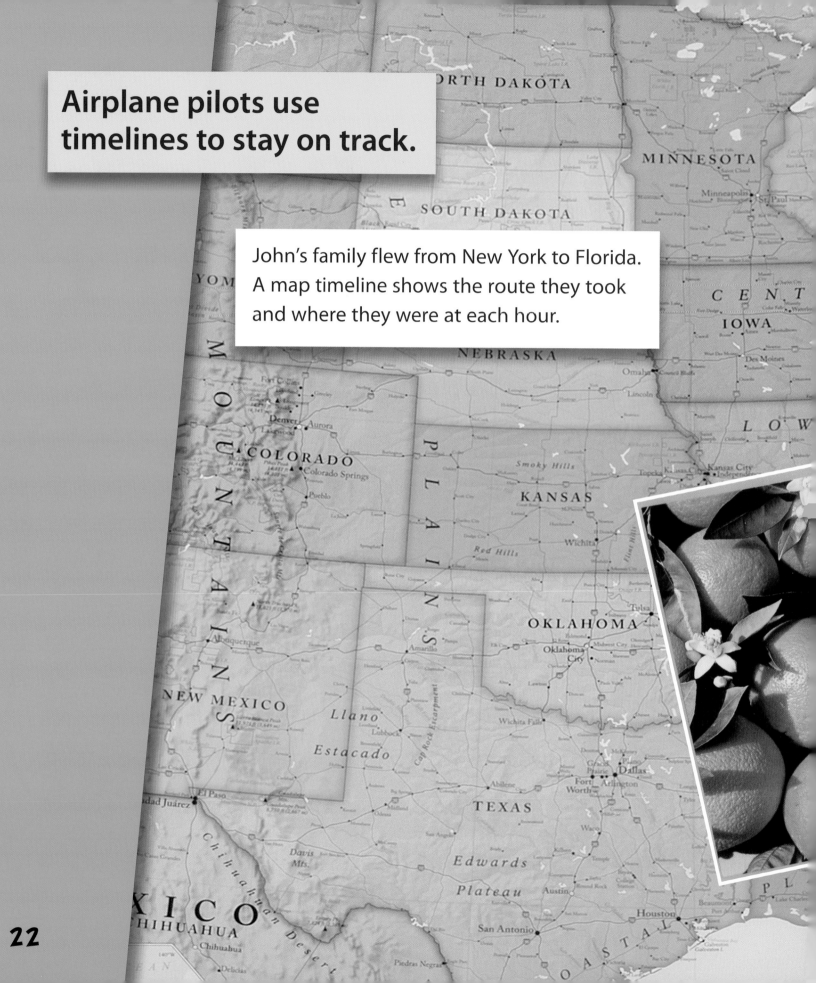

Airplane pilots use timelines to stay on track.

John's family flew from New York to Florida. A map timeline shows the route they took and where they were at each hour.

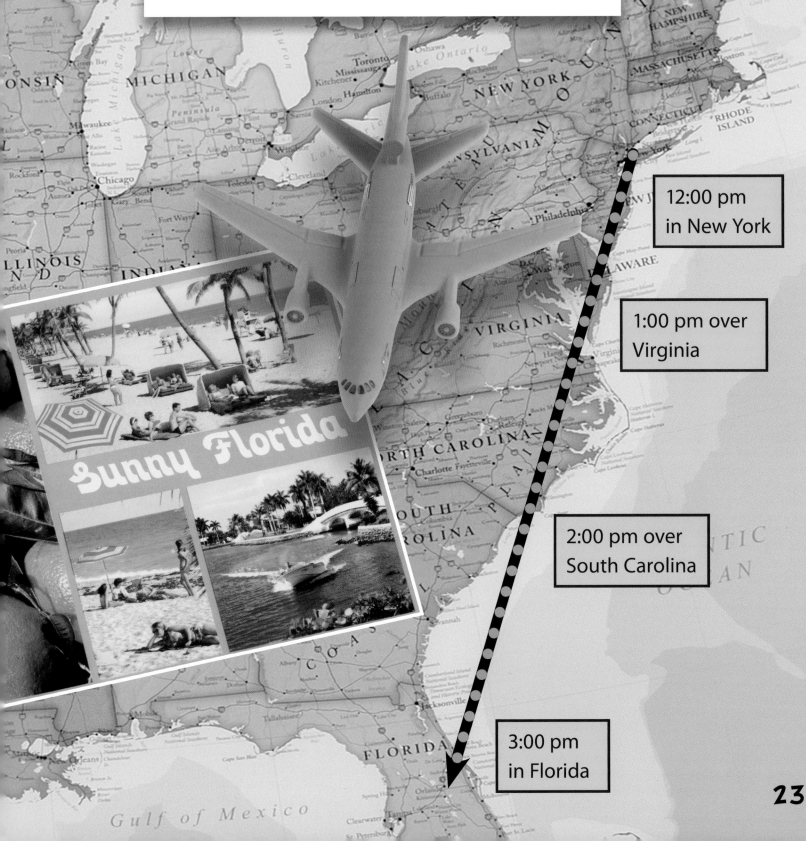

We can travel across the country in a few hours on an airplane!

12:00 pm in New York

1:00 pm over Virginia

2:00 pm over South Carolina

3:00 pm in Florida

Long ago there were no jet planes.

People found
other ways to fly.

This tabletop timeline uses objects to show how flying has changed over many years.

1783 hot air balloon

1903 airplane

1970 jumbo jet

1981 space shuttle

What do you think the next way to fly will be?

Living Timelines

Let's make a living timeline!

What order would you put these items in to make a timeline for the bean sprouts?

Which would be first?	Which would be second?
1.	2.

Finger trace each picture to a box to show their order.

Which would be last?

3.

There are many ways to make a timeline. You can take photos or draw pictures. You can use words. You can go up, across, or in a circle.

Happy Valentine's Day!

Presidents
Day

Independence
Day

You can even make a living
timeline with your friends!

Glossary

events—things that happen

journey—a trip

route—the way you take from one place to another

Critical Thinking Using the Common Core

1. Look at the timeline on pages 8 and 9. Did Deon do his homework before or after playing with his brother? Explain how you figured out your answer. (Key Ideas and Details)

2. Compare the circle timeline on pages 18 and 19 with the map timeline on pages 20 and 21. Do you think that one timeline provides more information than the other? Explain why or why not. (Craft and Structure)

3. Look at the children on pages 28 and 29. What could you show in a different living timeline? Explain how you would go about creating your timeline. (Integration of Knowledge and Ideas)

Read More

Davis, Todd, and Marc Frey. *The New Big Book of U.S. Presidents.* Philadelphia: Running Press Kids, 2008.

Miles, Liz. *Sports: From Ancient Olympics to the Super Bowl.* Timeline History. Chicago: Heinemann Library, 2011.

Spengler, Kremena. *An Illustrated Timeline of Transportation.* Visual Timelines in History. Mankato, Minn.: Picture Window Books, 2012.

Internet Sites

FactHound offers a safe, fun way to find Internet sites related to this book. All of the sites on FactHound have been researched by our staff.

Here's all you do:

Visit *www.facthound.com*

Type in this code: 9781476502618

 Check out projects, games and lots more at
www.capstonekids.com

Index

mL   1-14